"to gnaw." This is because all rodents have one pair of upper and one pair of lower incisor teeth at the front of their mouth. The incisors

Mice become very tame with regular handling.

grow continually and are worn down as they grind against each other as the rodent gnaws at its food.

Understanding Mice

Most of the mice that are kept as pets are domesticated mice. These are the same species as wild house mice, but have been selectively bred in captivity for many years to bring out the characteristics that are desirable in a domesticated animal. Other species are sometimes available, such as deer mice, which are similar in size but have a dark brown or sandy coat, a white underbelly, and white feet.

Mice become most active at dusk, and stay awake until the early hours of the morning. Although they do not form the same bond with their owners as larger rodents, such as rats, they can become very tame with regular handling. They will only bite if frightened or in pain, and although their nip may make your eyes water, it is unlikely to inflict any serious harm.

DID YOU KNOW?

Although we think of rodents as being small, the largest is the South American capybara, or water hog, that has a body length of about four feet (1.2 m) and can weigh more than 100 pounds (45 kg).

How Many?

In the wild, mice will sometimes live alone, but in captivity they are best kept in small groups. Two adult males together will invariably fight, and male mouse urine has a very strong "mousy" smell, so two females are the ideal combination, unless you want to breed.

Handling a Mouse

It is important that mice are handled regularly and gently from an early age, as they will then become very tame. Mice can be grasped by the base of their tail (close to the body) for restraint, but should not be held suspended upside down for any length of time. To hold your mouse securely for any procedure that may need to be carried out, place it on your sleeve, where it will instinctively hold on, and hold it by the scruff (the back of the neck) with the other hand.

DID YOU KNOW?

An adult mouse will eat approximately one-eighth of its body weight in food every day, which is the equivalent of a 160-pound (70-kg) man eating about 20 pounds (9kg) of food each day.

A mouse will instinctively hang on to a flat surface.

Living with Other Animals

Cats and small dogs, such as terriers, are predators that have been bred to kill rodents, so unless they have grown up in each other's company, it is very unlikely that they will be safe together.

Life Expectancy

Perhaps one of the main disadvantages of mice is their short life span – most will only live for a couple of years. Losing a pet is always tough – even if you know that its life expectancy is short – but at least you can have the satisfaction of knowing that you have given your mouse the best possible love and care.

Unlike many other animal species that have been domesticated, pet mice have kept the same basic body shape as their wild ancestors. The white mouse was originally bred for laboratory purposes, and this is still, by far, the most common color, but a large number of other varieties are available. If you thought that all mice are pretty much the same, you would soon be corrected by a member of the Mouse Fancy, people who expend a great deal of effort breeding their mice in an amazing variety of colors. For show purposes, these color patterns fall into four main groups:

Selfs

A single body color that can include black, blue, chocolate, fawn, cream, and silver.

Tans

Any of the self colors on the upper body, and tan on the underside.

Marked

White mice with different color patches on the body. Color patterns can be described as broken, even, variegated, Dutch, Himalayan, and tri-colored.

Any Other Variety

Includes all the other color and coat types, such as chinchilla, agouti, long-haired, and many more. Believe it or not, there are now even blue point Siamese mice, named after the Siamese cat with similar coloring.

There is very little difference between the varieties of domestic mice from the point of view of keeping them as pets. The choice is therefore very much one of personal preference, although the price should also be taken into account, as the unusual varieties will be more expensive.

A female house mouse starts to breed at six weeks of age and can have ten litters of about six young each year. If all the young survive and breed in turn, one pair of mice can produce half a million per year!

Most reputable pet shops sell mice, and the best will be able to offer advice on what to buy. Otherwise, you may know someone locally who breeds mice and possibly competes at shows, who may be able to help you. You might be able to find the address of a local breeder from your veterinarian or newspaper. You may also be able to obtain a pet from a friend who has bred some.

Look for a mouse that is clean and well cared for.

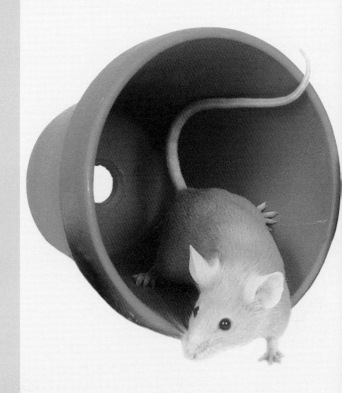

In all instances, look for a mouse that is clean and well cared for. In a pet shop, it is a good sign if the sales clerks are knowledgeable and can give you advice when you are making your choice. Resist the temptation to buy a sickly mouse from a pet shop just because you feel sorry for it – you could end up with a lot of heartache, trouble, and expense trying to get it well.

It is always best to buy pet mice when they are young, at about four weeks of age, because they are much easier to socialize and to train.

Female

What Sex Is My Mouse?

Sexing young mice can be tricky, but if they are compared side by side, the distance between the anus and the genital opening can be seen to be about twice as great in the male as the female. At two or three weeks of age, the nipples of a female mouse can be clearly seen before the hair tends to hide them. In adult mice, the testicles can be seen just below the anus.

Male

Signs of a Healthy Mouse

A healthy mouse should be bright and active, except when asleep during the day. Check the bottom of the cage for well-formed droppings. If you are looking for a good breeding specimen, it should have an elongated and lean body, tulip-shaped, upright ears, prominent eyes, and a long tail. The tail should be as long as the body, giving a total length of 7 to 8 inches (up to 20 cm).

Body condition:
Well covered and rounded. No abnormal swellings.

Coat:
Well groomed. Should not be soiled or matted.

Eyes:
Bright and clear, without any discharge.

Nose:
Clean and free of discharge.

Mouth:
Clean. Dribbling can be a sign of problems.

Breat
Quiet
regula
not be

10

The Journey Home

You will need to transport your mouse in a suitable carrier with some paper shavings for comfort. For a short journey, a sturdy cardboard box with a close-fitting lid pierced by ventilation holes is fine, but don't leave a mouse unattended in this sort of box for any length of time, as it will soon eat its way out!

Introducing a New Mouse

If you purchase a new mouse to add to an existing group, you should always keep it in strict isolation for a couple of weeks to make sure it is not incubating any diseases. It is then best to introduce the animals to each other outside the cage on neutral ground.

Skin:
*Pink and clean
on ears and tail.*

*ild
ed.*

Mice

Mice are creatures of the night, and there is nothing they dislike more than direct sunlight. (Okay, cats probably do come higher on the list of pet hates!) Their health is also likely to be adversely affected by dampness and drafts, so their housing needs to be snug, dry, and shaded.

Wire Cages

Mice love a nice piece of wood to chew on, so wooden cages are really not suitable. Some wooden cages are lined with wire mesh, but they are difficult to clean effectively. Metal cages are most widely used, although the bars must be suitably close together to prevent escape, and the lid must fit tightly. Most cages of this type have a plastic tray base that can be detached for easy cleaning.

A sleeping compartment is not essential if plenty of bedding is supplied, but many owners like to provide one, and a wide range of imaginative designs are available from pet stores.

DID YOU KNOW?

Baby mice use an ultrasonic cry, inaudible to the human ear, to call their mother back to the nest if they get cold or hungry. This is why some electronic equipment that emits ultrasonic radiation, such as television remote control units, can cause mice considerable distress.

A wire cage suitable for mice.

Glass Tanks

A glass tank is fine as an alternative to a cage, providing that it is well-ventilated and placed away from direct sunlight. The temperature should be between 60 and 80° Fahrenheit (15–27°C), since significantly higher temperatures can result in heatstroke. Each mouse needs at least 40 square inches (260 sq cm) of floor space, with a minimum floor area of about 18 x 12 inches (1200 cm), and a recommended height of at least 12 inches (30 cm) to reduce the chance of escape.

DID YOU KNOW?

A mouse's heart beats about 600 times every minute – or ten times a second.

Floor Covering

The floor covering should be of peat moss or wood shavings (make sure they haven't been treated with any preservatives). Supply plenty of bedding material in the form of hay, shredded paper, or biodegradable hamster bedding, as this will reduce the risk of fighting.

Wood shavings can be used as bedding material.

Water Bottle

Mice do not generally drink very much, especially if they eat significant amounts of succulent foods, such as cucumbers and lettuce, but they should always have a supply of fresh water available. This is best supplied with a gravity-fed drinking water bottle that can be suspended upside down in the cage or tank.

DID YOU KNOW?

The pet mouse is the same species of animal as the house mouse, *Mus musculus*.

Playtime for Mice

Providing a range of toys for your mice will help to keep them occupied, and make them much more entertaining as pets. Sometimes the cheapest toys are the best – so try giving your mice a present of the cardboard tube from inside a toilet paper roll, an empty cotton spool, or a cardboard egg box. They love climbing inside them and will come to no harm if they chew them up.

Mice also enjoy exercise wheels, ladders, pieces of piping to clamber through, and you can even construct an elaborate climbing frame. Check the design of any cage furnishing to make sure it cannot injure your mice, particularly if it is chewed.

DID YOU KNOW?

Mice have lived side by side with humans for around 10,000 years, originating in the grain-producing areas of northern Asia and spreading to all parts of the world.

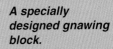

A specially designed gnawing block.

Playtime for Mice

Mice love to "work out" in their exercise wheel, but a mouse that spends too much time in its wheel is probably bored, and should be offered a wider variety of playthings.

Regular Exercise

Letting a pet rodent have free run of the house is a recipe for disaster, as they can easily get lost or injured, and love sharpening their teeth on electrical cords. However, you can bring your mice out of their home for regular exercise. This must be done under close supervision, ideally in a "playpen area."

A hidey-hole for mice.

Hand Training

When you get home, allow the new arrival to settle down alone in its cage with a supply of fresh food and water before you start hand-taming it. Even if you move its home later on, initially it should be situated in a quiet spot, away from hustle and bustle. Get the mouse used to the scent of your hand, and then tempt it with tasty treats to come to you. Mice learn quickly, and will soon come running to you, particularly if you start off feeding them entirely by hand.

The inside tube of a toilet paper roll makes a tunnel to explore.

A play ball should be used only for limited periods, always under your supervision.

Feeding

Ask anyone what a mouse eats, and the prompt reply will be "cheese!" In fact, mice are omnivorous, which means that in the wild they will eat pretty much whatever comes their way, be it meat or vegetable. It is important that mice have a diet that exercises their teeth and keeps them worn down – good-quality hard grains or leafy hay and grass will fulfill this function.

A Balanced Diet

A wild mouse may only live a matter of months, but a pet mouse should live for two or three years. A good diet will play a major role in increasing the chances of your pet enjoying a relatively long and healthy life. The ideal, balanced food for pet mice is one of the commercial diets that are designed to provide all their nutritional needs.

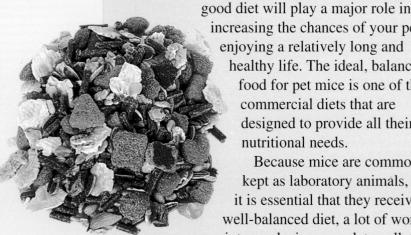

A commercial mouse food mix.

Because mice are commonly kept as laboratory animals, where it is essential that they receive a well-balanced diet, a lot of work has gone into producing complete pelleted foods for mice. These may seem boring, but they do ensure that the mouse cannot just pick out the morsels he fancies and leave the rest. Don't buy more than a two-month supply of food, and keep it in a dry, air-tight container. The food should be suspended in the cage in small wire baskets to prevent contamination.

Millet is appreciated in small quantities.

Mouse Nibbles

Commercial foods may supply the basic needs of a pet mouse, but a variety of food provides interest for both the animal and its owner, since we all get enjoyment from seeing the pleasure that a special treat may give our pets. Here are some of the things your mouse may safely munch. However, they should not make up more than 10 percent of the total diet.

• Millet or mixed budgerigar seeds
• Whole oats
• Greens and carrots – preferably not lettuce or celery
• Wholewheat toast – but go very easy on the butter
• Hardboiled egg, cheese, meat scraps – just a little from time to time, especially when rearing young

A supply of pelleted food can be left in the food bowls around the clock, but the best time to feed perishable foods is in the early evening, when the mice are most active. Uneaten remains can be removed before bedtime.

Supplements

If you are giving your mouse a varied diet, or a commercial food that is well balanced, there should be no need to add extra vitamins and minerals to the diet. If you are concerned that your pet may not be getting enough of these, especially at times when it needs extra, such as when it is growing, or rearing its young, a tiny pinch of a balanced small animal supplement can be sprinkled onto the food two or three times a week.

Caring for Your Mouse

Bedding should be changed two or three times a week.

There are no vaccinations that you can give your mouse to prevent disease, in the same way that you can with pet cats and dogs. Fortunately, mice are pretty sturdy, low-maintenance pets, and as long as they are provided with suitable food and housing as described in this book, problems are rare.

Cleaning the Cage

The bedding should be changed two or three times a week to minimize odors and reduce the risk of disease. The cage should be thoroughly cleaned out and disinfected every three or four weeks.

Caring for Your Mouse

Teeth

A mouse's teeth grow all the time, but normally they wear down naturally if there are plenty of things to gnaw on. A wooden block or a fruit tree branch (that hasn't been sprayed with insecticides) will help to keep the teeth in trim. Sometimes the teeth do not grow in proper alignment and they become overgrown. If this happens, the mouse will show signs of discomfort around the mouth and the teeth may then need regular cutting.

Nails

Mice generally keep their toenails short by digging and scrabbling around their cage. However, you should check them from time to time to make sure they do not need clipping, especially if the mouse is elderly. It is best to get a vet to show you how to clip nails and teeth. Nail clipping can then be carried out at home, using nail clippers. If you are a novice mouse keeper, you can ask someone who is more experienced to help. Cutting a nail too short will be painful and will result in bleeding, although this will soon stop if left alone.

Mice will groom their fur to keep it clean.

Arranging for a mixed sex group of

mice is pretty straightforward – the main problem is stopping them from breeding. For breeding purposes, mice are most commonly kept in trios of one male and two females. The female comes into heat every four or five days throughout the year from about two months of age, and the male matures sexually at a similar age. Pregnancy lasts about 20 days, and the female will build a nest when her young are due. It is important that she is left undisturbed for at least two or three days after giving birth, or she may turn on her young and eat them. Each litter will consist of an average of 10 youngsters, but litters of up to 16 can occur.

The mother should be left undisturbed for two or three days after she has given birth.

Breeding

The Young

Mice are born extremely immature, with no hair, and unable to hear or see. They develop quickly, however, with hair covering their body within ten days. They are

weaned and ready to leave the nest by three weeks of age.

Mother mouse needs very little human assistance during this stage, and interfering with her nest could cause her to eat her young. Just make sure she has a highly nutritious diet available, and let nature do the rest.

The male is a pretty lazy so-and-so who plays very little part in bringing up the young, but there is no need to separate the males from the mothers with their young. The female will come into heat again within about twenty-four hours of giving birth, and can have another litter immediately. However, this is a considerable drain on her resources, so it is best to allow her to rest for a while.

Leaving Your Mouse

Mice can safely be left alone for two or three days, as long as there is a good supply of food and water. Only a small amount of perishable food should be left. If you are away for a longer period, you may be able to board your mouse with a veterinarian, a pet shop, or perhaps a breeder.

Of course, a mouse is small enough to be moved easily to a friend or relative who may be prepared to look after it, or a neighbor may be prepared to make a daily visit for feeding and cleaning.

Make sure that whoever looks after your mouse knows all about its requirements. Leave the phone number of your veterinarian in case a problem should arise.

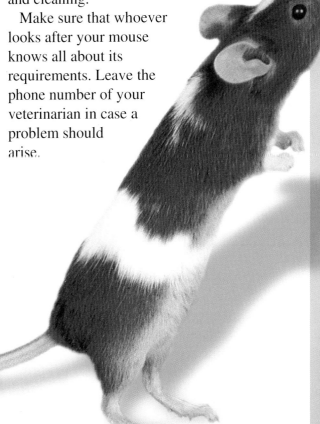

If you need to leave your mouse for a couple of days, make sure it has a good supply of food and water.

First Aid

The most important care for a sick or injured mouse is to keep it warm and administer fluids to try and prevent dehydration, which can occur quite quickly. A dropper or a small syringe is ideal for administering solutions, but do not use excessive force and remember that fluids can cause more harm than good if they are inhaled. Commercial rehydration powders, which are designed to be made up with water, can be purchased from a vet or a pharmacy, but a mouse will only take a few drops at a time. Alternatively, you can use boiled tapwater that has been allowed to cool, with a heaping tablespoonful of glucose powder and a level teaspoonful of salt per pint (just over half a liter) added.

Injuries

Small wounds can be gently flushed with warm water and treated with a mild antiseptic, but any major injuries will require veterinary attention. It is quite common for over-inquisitive mice to fall off a high surface. If this happens, the mouse should be gently returned to its nest to recover from the shock. If it does not improve within an hour, it may have broken some bones or suffered internal injuries, and will need to see a vet. Make sure the mouse is kept warm while in transit, as a drop in body temperature is often fatal.

Going to the Vet

If your mouse is seriously unwell, your veterinarian must be contacted without delay for assistance. Although children often care for mice, a responsible adult should to take the mouse to the vet and authorize any treatment needed.

Most small animal veterinary practices see a large number of small mammals and are very willing and able to treat them. It is even possible to anesthetize mice to carry out surgical operations, such as tumour removal or even amputation of a badly damaged limb, although the risks are greater than for a cat or a dog undergoing a similar procedure.

Treating Mice

Few pharmaceuticals have been developed and tested for use in mice, because the market is simply not big enough to make it financially viable for a drug company. Therefore a vet has to use products that are available for other animal species, or even human medicines. This makes the use of any drug more unpredictable in mice than in many other animals.

Administering medications to a mouse can be difficult, although it can sometimes be managed with drops of a liquid medicine that can be given orally or added to some food. A mouse may refuse to drink water that has been treated, particularly when it is unwell. A course of injections is often the safest way to ensure that a mouse receives proper treatment, but it does involve repeated visits to the vet.

Common Ailments

There is a wide range of diseases that have been reported in mice, but very few of them are common in those kept in small groups as pets. Those of most importance include:

Abscesses

Fighting is not uncommon, especially between male mice, and the small puncture wounds that result can easily become infected and develop into abscesses. These can be seen either as hard, hot, and tender swellings or patches of hair loss and skin ulceration. The affected area needs to be cleaned up with a skin preparation, and usually antibiotic treatment is necessary.

Respiratory Disease

Respiratory infections are common, and underlying causes can include poor ventilation, dusty cage bedding, or dirty flooring that holds in ammonia from the urine.

All mice have a range of potentially harmful bacteria and viruses in their lungs, but the mouse's immune system keeps them under control. However, they get a chance to multiply and cause disease problems if the mouse's natural resistance is lowered by poor hygiene, inadequate diet, illness, injury, or just old age. The

mouse will show symptoms, such as sneezing, red and watery eyes, and labored breathing.

Treatment with antibiotics may help the problem, particularly if only the upper airways are affected, but it is often more a matter of control rather than cure. The outlook for a mouse with pneumonia (infection of the lungs) is very poor.

Diarrhea

This is another common condition affecting pet mice. It can be due to a variety of causes, such as infection by bacteria, protozoa (single-celled organisms), or parasites such as roundworms and tapeworms. Sudden changes in diet, or the feeding of food that has gone rancid or moldy, can also trigger a digestive upset.

Mild cases will often respond to conservative treatment, such as removing all perishable foodstuffs from the diet and simply feeding a complete, dry food. In more serious or longer lasting cases, a veterinarian may want to have a fecal sample analyzed in order to establish the cause. Occasionally, mice can be infected with an organism that can be passed on to people, such as salmonella, commonly associated with human food poisoning. Strict hygiene, including keeping pet mice away from food preparation areas, and hand washing after handling, is always advisable, but especially if your mouse has been showing signs of digestive disturbance.

A serious case of diaarrhea is a symptom of Tyzzers disease, a bacterial infection that is almost always fatal. It can be triggered if the mouse's immune system is lowered by being kept in poor conditions or by being otherwise stressed.

Skin Problems

It is possible for mice to suffer from ringworm, a fungus that grows on the hairs and can also cause skin problems in humans and other animals. This is usually seen as patches of hair loss, with scaliness of the underlying skin, especially around the head. Mice can also be infected by mites, which either live on the surface of the skin or burrow deeper into it. Mites tend to cause quite a lot of irritation, and can be diagnosed by a vet by taking a scraping from the skin.

In the case of either fungal or parasitic

infections of the skin, it is usually necessary for a vet to prescribe a medicated shampoo for treatment. Sometimes mice kept in groups gnaw off each other's whiskers, a practice rather quaintly called "barbering."

Cancer

This is very common in older mice, occurring in many possible sites around the body. Mammary (breast) growths are frequently seen, and are usually malignant. They tend to recur or spread to other parts of the body even if surgically removed.

Eye Problems

Conjunctivitis, causing soreness of the eyes, is not uncommon in mice. It can be initiated by a more generalized problem, such as a respiratory infection, or by irritation of the eyes by dust particles. A veterinarian will be able to prescribe antibiotic drops to treat the problem.

Poisoning

Mice are quite sensitive to poisoning, particularly because they spend a lot of time grooming and will lick off any substances that get onto their coat. Take great care not to use any aerosol sprays in the room in which the mouse lives without checking first to make sure they are nontoxic to animals.